ILZE'S DAUGHTER

A Latvian Childhood in Pennsylvania

poems by

Livija Rieksts Bolster

Finishing Line Press
Georgetown, Kentucky

ILZE'S DAUGHTER

A Latvian Childhood in Pennsylvania

For my children and their children
Par atmiņu—maniem bērniem un mazbērniem

Copyright © 2024 by Livija Rieksts Bolster
ISBN 979-8-88838-755-9 First Edition
All rights reserved under International and Pan-American Copyright Conventions. No part of this book may be reproduced in any manner whatsoever without written permission from the publisher, except in the case of brief quotations embodied in critical articles and reviews.

ACKNOWLEDGMENTS

Thank you to the Inkfingers, indomitable writers (Deb, Kaaren, Carla, Kate, Paul, Sheila) who urged me to write from my heart, to share the story of my family. The courage my parents possessed to step into a strange new world gave me courage to articulate emotions and experiences long held guarded. Thank you, Seema for giving me a safe space for my first public reading. Thanks to poets Memye Curtis Tucker and Rupert Fike for their encouragement and sound advice. Special thanks to my husband, Paul, and my immediate family for their never waning support. *Paldies.*

Publisher: Leah Huete de Maines
Editor: Christen Kincaid
Cover Art: Livija Rieksts Bolster
Author Photo: Nathan Bolster
Cover Design: Elizabeth Maines McCleavy

Order online: www.finishinglinepress.com
also available on amazon.com

Author inquiries and mail orders:
Finishing Line Press
PO Box 1626
Georgetown, Kentucky 40324
USA

Contents

Ilze's Daughter 1

Bad Boys Lose Out 2

Don't Ask Me 4

If Only I Could 6

My Latvian World 8

Jura Bango 9

Hiyo Silver Away 10

Home 11

Friday Nights 12

Mama's Piragi 14

Week Adrift 16

Papa 17

Sibling Torture 18

Sadie Hawkins Day 19

In the Same Country 20

Latvian Baptists Don't Dance, I Was Told 22

Life Interrupted 23

To Rise Again 25

Now, Then 27

Fragile Memory 30

Addendum 32

ILZE'S DAUGHTER

runt of the litter
failure to thrive
returned to hospital
prayed back to life in an upper room
I am Ilze's daughter
fifth child within ten years
granddaughter of Katrina

born in 1876, Katrina
owned a farm in Latvia
bore four children
survived three husbands
died in refugee flight
before we could meet

how little do I know
of Ilze's early life
bits, pieces, snatches of stories
like crumbs left on a plate
formal sepia photos hint
a life of plenty, hired help
chefs sent out from Riga
for three-day wedding feast—
bits, pieces, snatches of stories
tinged with grief, loss
of once upon a time

yet, strength surges through—
she weathered soldiers' boots scarring
wooden kitchen floor
refused scarce life vests if
her children were without
fled threat of Russian control once more
west over mountains to the free zone
then further west
to begin anew

I am Ilze's daughter
runt of the litter
prayed back to life in an upper room
granddaughter of Katrina

BAD BOYS LOSE OUT

I wanted to be daring!
I wanted to be wild.

But I was an Alpha girl, fresh
from weeding my family's vegetable garden,
raking hay, baking *piragi*, walking
to Saturday School to learn
Latvian grammar and history.

They,
were the boys of Lambda,
outstanding athletes,
the daring ones,
bad boys.

They were credited with stealing
the statue of Holy Mother Mary from Cabrini College,
a school for Catholic girls just across Eagle Road,
boundary road between
two opposing Christian schools,
the road, where glowing
just-off-campus cigarettes
sparked winter nights.

They deposited the Holy Mother
into one of our Baptist campus lakes
to swim with the ducks and Canada geese,
whose activities enlivened
after-dinner walks of couples—
especially during mating season—
theirs and ours.

They were accused of scrawling "Cyril Saves"
over the many-layered paint on The Rock,
bearer of student messages over the years.
No one admitted deifying Cyril, Dean of Students.
The Holy Mother was fished out, returned
to her Catholic campus home.
Yet, any freshman girl would be impressed
if a Lambda boy turned his eyes towards her.

I wanted to be that freshman girl.
I wanted to be daring,
I wanted to be wild.

It was a Zeta man who captured
my attention, his mind full
of questions, questions, questions.
Armored with humor
and persistence, his love
just wouldn't let me go.

DON'T ASK ME

Don't ask me.
I really can't say
if fear surged up suffocating
mother so breath came only
in gasps
as she climbed
onto an overloaded wagon,
gripped its unforgiving seat with one hand,
clutched her baby with the other
as they lurched
over worn roads to
faint hope of refuge.

Don't ask me.
I really can't say
how father made the quick decision
to turn towards the sea,
avoiding blockade after blockade
on those war-rutted roads. Perhaps
a ship was heading to sea
before roaring war planes dropped
their deadly loads. Perhaps
under cover of doused lights
the ship could slip
oh-so-carefully past underwater mines.

Don't ask me why
now mother
sits on a solitary chair,
head in hands,
moaning and crying. Nothing
father says comforts her.

Don't ask me.
I really can't say
how I know
it is barns left filled with harvest,
cows moaning to be milked,
apples soldiers will snatch,
her beloved *Simani*,
childhood home, abandoned.

It is friends, siblings, no longer
to meet at garden gate,
it is whispering birch trees, pale peeling
skins, breeze-gentled, she will see again,
only in her dreams.
Don't ask me.

IF ONLY I COULD

Ilze waits for news
of her brother Jēkabs.
Month after month
week after week
day after day
no word.

Katrina, her mother,
who fled with the family
died in their German exile.
Teodors, her stepfather, stayed
behind, cancer quickly taking him.
Brother Matīz succumbed to a fever.
Līze, her half-sister, joined her in America.

That left only Jēkabs, proud
in his cap and leather jacket,
chauffeured high ranking officials. *"I'll
be fine,"* he assured her, as he kissed
her goodbye in Liepaja, as panic-filled she
quickly boarded the last ship leaving port.

First Germany, one DP camp,
then another, another.
Five years later she reached
the promised land:
United States of America,
streets of gold, safety,
a new life.

Finally, the mailbox brings good news—
a letter in Jēkabs' handwriting.
Yes, I'm doing fine.
I'm healthy, I have work.
So glad you're in America. It must
be wonderful there. You must be doing well,
safe and prosperous. I'm only sad
my leather jacket was destroyed in the fires
from the bombing. Could you
send me a new one?

Could you send me a new one? Her
breath catches,
tears come quickly.
Oh,
I wish that I could.

Her mean circumstances,
her inability
to grant one
simple wish
washes out all her joy.

Sad, embarrassed,
she whispers again, *Oh,*
If only I could.
She wipes her tears, folds
the letter, and tucks it away
in a bottom drawer.

MY LATVIAN WORLD

Glossy, wide, white ribbon
tied in a large bow perches
on top of my straight
brown hair pulled up off my forehead.
Round little nose, rosebud mouth,
petite frame still carrying baby roundness in my limbs.
I sit politely,
hands folded in my lap,
in the row of other be-ribboned girls. The one
next to me, a distant cousin,
boasts a bounty of wonderful, blond curls,
a new full-skirted dress. Behind us
are the young boys in miniature woolen suits,
short pants, knee socks, old-country woven string ties.
A formal Sunday photograph, its sepia tones
stop time inside the capsule of a small wooden church
on the outskirts of a Pennsylvania village.

For a short while, this was my world—
playing games
in the church yard on work-days,
reciting Latvian poems at Christmas programs,
blending my struggling alto
with voices in the church choir.
This was
where I brought my American fiancé
to say our vows in two languages.

This was
where I watched my father,
pushing his walker
as he followed my mother's casket
down the short aisle
out the church door.

JURA BANGO!*
   translated Storming Sea

Visitors were rare
to the two-story stucco house surrounded
by fields of oats
gardens of raspberries, strawberries
sugar beets, potatoes
grape arbor, chickens
stone well and pump
of course, path to the outhouse,

Visitors were rare
discouraged by hole-pocked dirt lane
houseful of children, seven,
four girls, three boys
almost enough for a baseball team.

We took turns
pressing our ear to
metal grate set in bedroom floor, straining
to identify voices in living room below.
Stretched out, turning
to just the right angle
we could see the visitor,
inevitably, disappointingly,
minister or church member.

We would gather in the grass
of a firefly-filled evening
take our bases, bare-footed, glove-less
to play our own game—*Jura Bango.*
A strolling leader created a story, weaving
in each player's chosen word, the signal
for each to join the pied piper. Bases now empty
the leader abruptly ended the story shouting, *Jura Bango!*
sending us skittering
back to safety of bases
before they were occupied—
our version of
Musical Chairs, outdoors.

HI-YO SILVER AWAY

Spectacularly jaunty,
a miniature Annie Oakley
(though I had no idea
who she was)
leather belt, well,
hard plastic *pleather*, I guess,
slung around my thin five-year-old hips,
pair of silver guns
jutting from holsters.

Memory paints an idyllic day,
warm sun, birthday fortune,
does not recall
the gift-giver.
Did they know the status
their gift would bestow?
I stood taller, leaner, meaner,
confidently challenging my
older siblings.

We played through afternoon's
shadows, stalking each other
behind tobacco leaves,
chicken shed, secret spaces
under the porch.
Dusk darkened my world.
Time for one last turn
around the far end
of the tobacco field before
loping home to dinner.

Too late I sensed
an empty holster,
one silver gun now buried
under foliage, killing
half my swagger.

HOME

We called them the Rockies,
huge boulders, as if
some god
scattered them
among the trees
just for us
to climb, skin our knees.

The open meadow,
mowed by our feet,
was perfect,
a baseball field
for seven children and neighbors.
The cavernous barn, stuffed with hay,
held enticing lofts and ladders for games
more complicated than hide and seek.
The lilac bush sent its intoxicating spell
across the yard, reeling
into our senses so we
would never forget home.

Grown, I returned
to the house near the woods,
an urge to discover a new family
experiencing new adventures.
The house stood vacant.

My Rockies were large stones I
could easily circumvent;
my meadowed-baseball field shrank
to driveway size;
the barn was just a barn,
dilapidated building holding
no secrets.
But ahh, the lilac bush,
the lilac bush reeled
out its spell so I
could not forget home.

FRIDAY NIGHTS

We sardined into the old gray Nash
for the weekly trip to town.
Papa, well-worn suit jacket over work clothes—
always the jacket,
like in the old country—
walked into the bank, cashed
his check from the pants factory,
paid the mortgage,
and stopped at the Pennsylvania Power and Light
to pay the electric bill.

Then we headed
to the Q-Mart, long, low building
slung across hard gravel lot, bursting with
stall after stall of goods—
ready-made clothes, toys, furniture, knick-knacks.

Father started at the essential end,
vegetables, eggs and meat stands
of chickens, pork, ground beef, pigs' feet,
sausages, livers, scrapple.
Stanley Beidler, our school bus driver,
and minister at the local
Mennonite Church
ran the family farmstand.
They are people of faith, Papa noted
 this important fact.
Their vegetables were always freshly picked,
baskets heaped high,
chickens young, plump.
While Father bought staples, we tore
down aisles poking into stalls,
longing for a time
we could afford
that totally unnecessary toy,
a new, non-hand-me-down sweater.

Before heading home
we made one last stop,
the white, two-story house guarded
by a soaring pine tree, home to

the Latvian baker, Mr. Gedrovič.
Tall, gray-haired, flour-dusted, he
baked the sweet-sour (*saldskab*) maize
of our homeland we savored
sliced thin, toasted,
slathered with real butter,
on mornings before school, sometimes
sausage on the side.

But the guilty pleasure
in the dark back seat of our car
was the voraciously-torn
piece by hunk
still-warm long loaf
of French bread.
My sister favored
the crust. I dug
fingers deep into
the soft belly of the loaf,
each morsel ahh-melting in my mouth
until, tires crunched
the gravel drive of home.
Gone—
the bread,
the delicious moment.

MAMA'S PĪRAGI

Pungent, sweet odors float
upstairs
agitating
my senses. It's Saturday.

I feel cool
linoleum under bare feet
stepping into the kitchen,
center of alchemy. Baking Day.

The small room already
warm, apple pie
in the oven, large pot
center stage
on the white enamel table
waits Mama's chemistry,
earthy yeast, warm water.
Fermentation.

Flour, water, shortening,
nutmeg, cardamon, just
a hint of sugar.
Amounts? No paper recipe,
gleaning mine by jotting
approximations as Mama
constructs from remembered
repetition.

Tactile heaven, hands
plunging, kneading the mixture.
Mama instructs
The dough should fall off your hands.
Set aside, towel-covered,
Let it rise.

Soon Mama dips her hand into
plump pillows of dough, drops
a dollop on the floured spot
in front of me. Ready?

Years later,
You must work quickly, I say
to my daughter. *Watch.*
I stretch a corner of the baby-cheek-soft
dough, scoop in meat filling,
fold it over, with one swift move
of the metal cup,
pinch it off. Perfect crescent.

The smooth metal cup fits
my hand, familiar,
from Mama's kitchen in Pennsylvania,
Mama's kitchen in Latvia,
marked with scratched initials,
my name too etched into the side.
Livija Rieksts.

WEEK ADRIFT

All night long
the wind caressed
persistent snow, urging
it across open fields
filling up country roads
isolating us in our homes.
No cars, no milk man's truck
no mailman
no school bus.

For a week we snuggled
warm and safe. Each night
the wind took charge.
By day, cold blue skies teased
us outside in layers of sweaters,
rain boots, mittens, to stomp
through thigh-high drifts.
Mama sent us to get milk,
the farm a mile away.
It's a good day for a walk.

Glorious day! Milk
brought home, we took
to steep hills across the street
piling onto wooden sleds, clutching
each other for one more ride.
Dumping in joyful tumble
snow up our sleeves, under our jackets,
down our necks, only
to climb to the top
do it again.

PAPA

Once a year
Papa came home
from the pants factory early,
paper grocery bag in hand.
We knew it held magic—
Breyers ice cream, Hires root beer,
Wise potato chips.
His solitary week off marked our
summer vacation. We

accompanied him to
his off-time work,
caretaker for Mr. Bernstein's
home. The drive
up to the house, *Vagabond Farm*, curved
through countryside always
lush, green. A stone wall
protected manicured lawn,
extensive patio, step-stone entrance. Papa

began at the hulking red
barn, got his tools—wheelbarrow,
shovel, hoe, hand scythe, rake—
to cultivate numerous flower beds. Off
we went running down hills,
dipping feet in cold
creek water. The New York City
owner, extra Bentley, Mercedes tucked
in his garage, was only an occasional
visitor. No danger

of chastisement. Reveling
in pleasure of picnic lunches
on sweet hillsides, we were oblivious
to father's labor, sweat. Papa
was our provider, mesmerizing
teller of Latvian folk tales, our hero. Taken
for granted until his years-later fall
from a roof, agony-filled hours on unforgiving
ground. Papa recovered. Still
muscular, strong, still
the breadwinner, still our hero. No
longer invincible.

SIBLING TORTURE

cool air
wrapped around us
mosquitoes danced
on bare arms
grass still warm
on a July evening
in Pennsylvania
countryside

conspirators.
we squatted
behind the peonies, whispered
what do you think they're doing?
talking? about what?
kissing?
perhaps we knew, someday
we too would do the same

we belly-crawled
closer to the gravel driveway
parked Ford sedan
where two figures leaned
towards each other

we gathered pebbles
pinging them against
car door, window, roof
they ignored us
so we pinged again, again, again

we felt them stirring, peering
seeking us in the dark
we giggled in triumph
of secrecy and torture
of our older sister

the back door of the house flew open
a quick switch
flooded the yard with light

all too sudden
our mother
ended our delight

SADIE HAWKINS DAY

The tangle
of bud-tipped branches
stretched
too high
to climb.
Yet
a cast-wrapped foot swung
silently,
jubilantly from a limb.
You have to catch me first,
came a teasing voice from
the curly-haired boy.

*I can't reach you. There's
something I want to ask.*

You have to catch me first,
the voice challenged,
green eyes twinkled,
Those are the rules.

*How did you . . . ?
Could you . . . ?
Would you come down
to me?*
she asked, not-quite pleading.

*How long are you willing
to wait?* he parried.

She walked away.

Fifty years later she remembers
a ladder
carried to the tree,
the question asked,
answered.

As long as it takes, as long as it takes.

IN THE SAME COUNTRY

Papa
opened the Bible
in his lap,
travel-worn,
from the old country, words
in his native tongue, his name
inscribed: *Voldemars*.

We,
all nine of us, gathered
in the small living room—
one couch, some on the floor,
chairs drug in from
the dining room. It was

Christmas Eve.
The four-dollar tree stood
by the window, colored lights
sending bubbles up glass
cylinders. A few, very few
baubles. Wrapped gifts, few,
but enough, strewn underneath.
It was the night before

Christmas Day service
before our community gathered
 to celebrate the children's program—
struggling piano duets,
sibling skits involving an argument
resolved with giant gingerbread heart,
poems nervously recited from memory.

That evening
in the living room, our presentations
to our parents were a prelude,
prelude to opening gifts,
prelude to the story Papa read,
a story we knew by heart.

In later years
the tradition continued,
gifts opened Christmas Eve,
the story read, now
accompanied by a translation
for the American guest,
who likely also knew it by heart.

*And there were in the same
country, shepherds abiding.*

LATVIAN BAPTISTS DON'T DANCE, I WAS TOLD
reflections on attending the XV Latvian Song and Dance Festival

Four abreast they strode,
several hundred strong,
backs straight,
booted and slippered feet in step,
long skirts swirling,
deep reds, forest greens, rich blues, muted grays
vested bodices and chests,
long-sleeved flowing white shirts.

They covered the floor,
wave after wave in a sea of
colors, headdresses,
flying beribboned braids.
The music skirled, they
moved as one,
swaying, bending
stepping in a Latvian folk dance
I knew existed
but had never witnessed.

Voices with the music—
folk songs,
words I recognized,
but could not sing by heart.
My countrymen and women,
my language,
familiar, yet unfamiliar
as if peering through a scrim.

I now saw a splendid panoply of my heritage
I had only known in part.

LIFE INTERRUPTED

A friend found the list
at the accident site
in the village—
upturned Soviet jeep
driver dead in the road
military papers strewn.

Father's name on the orders
to be sent away next
sent to bitter Siberia,
like Viktors, the wealthy landowner—
five hundred acres
five servants
house full of fine furniture—
taken middle of the night
still dressed in nightclothes.

No one knows
what happened to him
not even a note
to his pregnant wife.
Their baby born blue
blue and cold
lifeless
like Siberia.

The decision
was made desperately,
the decision to leave everything
everything—
Sīmaņi, the family farm
an apple orchard, harvested fields
the familiar kitchen turned field hospital
stained with blood that will not wash away,

where limbs had been sawed
to save the life
of the blond German lieutenant, who
screamed until the pain took
his breath away. Breathless,
the decision to leave was made.

Tomorrow
we must leave.
Tomorrow
we will heave
two hand-built wooden boxes
onto the wagon
hitch up our best horses.
Tomorrow
we will whisper,
Goodbye, *Ardievu*.

Tonight
we must pack.

TO RISE AGAIN

The path takes Ilze
up the hill where white birches
newly-leaved whisper
of summer coming.
With a switch she lightly,
urges the cows
toward green pastures.
This is her farm, her home
where she entertained
wedding guests from Riga,
chased toddlers among
wild cherry trees, walked woods,
basket in hand, seeking
succulent mushrooms, flung
down blankets for meadow picnics.

This was her home.
Her eyes open. She
knows it was
but a dream
of her homeland.
Heart aching
she silently weeps.

She slips out of bed
in awakening day
loads wood into the stove,
brings water from outside pump,
begins breakfast for her family.

Later she sits on the stoop
washing diapers by hand, singing
ancient folk songs, *Strauji, strauji upe tecēj,*
in the comfortable old language.
She has difficulty with the new one.

Buffered by English-fluent children,
among strangers
she smiles a lot,
a shy, gentle, head down-tilted smile
and a soft *sank-you.*

At day's end she
has cooked and cleaned
planted and weeded
picked and pickled.

The dream will come again
that night
and the next. Again
she will weep.
With morning light
again she will rise.

NOW, THEN

Come, look, you said,
beckoning me
into the garden, bare feet
on damp grass. With exquisite
gentleness
you scooped
the sun-warmed nest
onto your open palm.
As you held the fur-naked babies
not quite rabbits
in your hands, outstretched but for
the one finger, taut tendon
frozen crooked,

Did your hands
remember
the smooth skin you caressed
as you nudged the cow into place
for milking? Did
your hands remember
gripping in tight panic
the infant in arms
as the wagon jostled away
in flight from
your home?

Come quickly, you said.
*It looks
like rain.* Together
we ran outside, pulling
wash from the clothesline, burying
noses in air-fresh scent.
As you carried
armfuls,
children's clothes, work shirts,

Did your arms
remember
smooth satin sliding, a gauzy
veil studded with myrtle sprigs,
tenderly folded, shelved away, not

to be carried
in the panicked journey
from *Sīmaṇi*?

Don't look, you warned.
I averted my eyes
from the black and white
screen where
clubs rained
down on human flesh,
hoses threw
young black bodies
to concrete sidewalks,
as tears rolled
down your cheeks.

Did your eyes
remember soldiers
shooting the innocent
druggist dragged from
his house? Did
you avert your eyes
as you pulled away from
your home,
not daring,
like Lot's wife,
to look back?

Come, you hold him
I invited,
handing you my firstborn. He
yawned and nestled
into your arms,
as you tenderly rocked.
You smiled.

Did your arms
remember
when you cradled each
of your own, stroking

love into their brows?
Did you remember glowing
with pride, sitting
in school auditoriums, programs
spoken in the new language honoring
your children, nurtured
in your new
American home?

FRAGILE MEMORY

I finger the image
my mind slowly calling out
questions I never asked
pulling at fragile yarn of memory
or a story told and retold?

Cool spring morning
close clustered houses
scratchy woolen tights hugging
fat little limbs
back and forth
strokes of wooden broom
sweeping a sidewalk of a city—
Greven, Germany?

Medicine
dripped onto tooth,
tasting brown, strong
yet sweet
on my tongue
pain-swollen cheek
scarf-smothered
sweater-on-sweater body
sleeping in warmth
of upstairs neighbor's cot.

I know this memory is real
this story true.
I have a photograph.

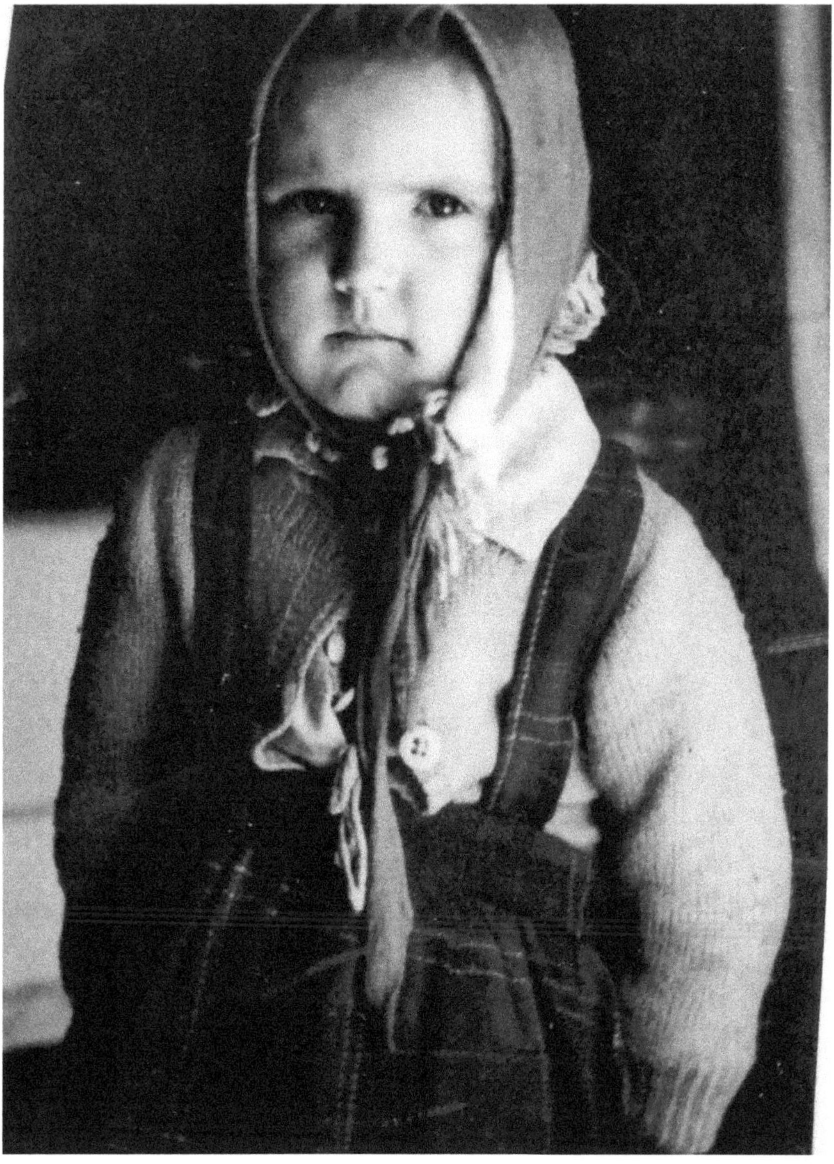

ADDENDUM

Six months after Adolf Hitler committed suicide, and three months after Japan surrendered officially ending World War II, I was born in Germany in a British displaced persons (DP) camp of Latvian parents. War had surrounded my family and war brought me to America's shores. I am now an American citizen, but at my core I am Latvian.

1871—Fricis Rieksts is born (my paternal grandfather)

1879—Katrina Ozoliņš is born (my maternal grandmother)

    1904-1905—Latvian uprising crushed by Russians

1908 or 1911—*Sīmaņi*, farm deeded to Katrina Ozolinš

1908—Ilze Palevics Rieksts, my mother, is born

1910—Voldemars Rieksts, my father, is born

    1914—1918—World War I—area of the Baltics is fought over by Germans and Russians
    1918—1939—Latvia is an independent state

1932—Katrina sold *Sīmaņi* to my mother, Ilze

1935—Ilze and Voldemars Rieksts are married

    1936—Nazi Germany and Fascist Italy sign cooperation treaty
    August, 1939—Nazi-Soviet Pact, a non-aggression treaty divided Eastern Europe. A Secret Protocol signed independent Latvia (along with Estonia, Lithuania, Finland and Romania) to Russia.

August 27, 1939—my sister, Ausma is born

    September, 1939—Germany invades Poland; Great Britain and France declare war on Germany. Soviet Union invades Poland from east.
    April—June 9, 1940—Germany invades Denmark, Norway
    June 14-18, 1940—Stalin invades Baltic States and begins reign of terror. Between 1940 and 1941, 40,000 Latvians

> *are deported to Siberia or killed. The three countries are annexed as Soviet Republics (USSR)*
>
> *May—June 22, 1940—Germany attacks western Europe; one after another the countries fall—France, Luxembourg, the Netherlands, Belgium*
>
> *July 10—October 31, 1940—the Battle of Britain*

January 25, 1941—my brother, Edvīns is born

> **June—November, 1941—Nazi terror replaces Soviet terror as Germany overruns the Baltic States and attacks Russia (Operation Barbarosa, siege of Leningrad)**
>
> *December, 1941—Soviet counteroffensive drives Germany from Moscow suburbs in retreat*
>
> *December 7, 1941—Japan bombs Pearl Harbor; December 8—U.S. declares war on Japan; Nazi Germany and Axis partners declare war on United States.*

May 29, 1942—my sister, Zenta is born

> *June, 1942—February, 1943—new German offensive met by Soviet counterattack*

November 20, 1943—my brother, Oskars is born

> *June, 1944—British and U. S. troops land on Normandy; by August, Allies reach Paris*
>
> **October 12, 1944—Riga (Latvia's capital) falls to USSR, followed by a bitter battle over Latvian territory, especially in the region where my parents lived at "Sīmaņi"**

October 14, 1944— Rieksts family leaves Sīmaņi. The family escapes on a ship evacuating wounded German soldiers, sailing out of Liepaja, Latvia

October 19, 1944—ship Gotenhafen lands in Danzig, Poland

November 11, 1944—Rieksts family is sent to Egeln, Germany in compulsory employment

> *April 30, 1945—Hitler commits suicide; May 7—Germany surrenders, Potsdam Conference divides Germany into four zones: France, Britain, U. S. and Russia*

July, 1945—Rieksts family, realizing they would be in Russian zone, escape to British zone (Camp Wuppertal-Langerfeld), then Greven, about 159 miles away

September 2, 1945—Japan surrenders. End of World War II.

October, 1945—1949—Rieksts family stays in DP Camp Greven (near Münster)

November 12, 1945—Livija Marta Rieksts (Riki Bolster) is born

July 17, 1949—family emigrates to USA via air from Camp Wentorf, Hamburg, London to Hartford, Connecticut

Family travels by train to Lillington, North Carolina (near Dunn) where sponsoring family lived

August 9, 1949—my sister, Mērija is born (22 days after we landed)

Fall of 1950—Rieksts family moved to Pennsylvania near a community of Latvians

April 1, 1952—my brother, Jānis is born

September 6, 1991, Soviet Union recognizes the independence of Latvia.

Born in Greven, Germany in a displaced persons camp, **Livija Rieksts Bolster** (Riki) emigrated to the United States in 1949. She grew up in rural Pennsylvania as part of a close-knit Latvian immigrant community. Much of her writing speaks to these experiences. She holds a BA in English from Eastern University and an M. Ed in Special Education from the University of Georgia.

A former journalism teacher, Riki Bolster taught for nineteen years at Grady High School (now Midtown H.S.), an inner-city school in Atlanta, Georgia. She developed and taught courses in Mass Media, Introduction to Journalism, Newspaper Production and Television Production. Her students and the student newspaper, *The Southerner,* consistently won state and national awards. She was named Atlanta Public Schools High School Teacher of the Year in 1998-99.

Upon retirement, Bolster created and coordinated the Grady High School Writing Center, a part-time, after-school program which encouraged students to enjoy the writing experience. The Center provided not only tutoring in writing assignments across disciplines, but also sponsored writing competitions, local author talks, and workshops in college essay writing, poetry and play-writing.

Bolster has published feature stories in neighborhood newspapers and written presentations for All About Developmental Disabilities. She served as first editor of *Saving the Georgia Coast,* published by the University of Georgia Press, 2020. *Ilze's Daughter* is her first book of poetry.

Milton Keynes UK
Ingram Content Group UK Ltd.
UKHW030853131024
449481UK00005B/235